LIBRARY AS PUBLISHER

Charleston Briefings: Trending Topics for Information Professionals is a thought-provoking series of brief books concerning innovation in the sphere of libraries, publishing, and technology in scholarly communication. The briefings, growing out of the vital conversations characteristic of the Charleston Conference and *Against the Grain*, will offer valuable insights into the trends shaping our professional lives and the institutions in which we work.

The *Charleston Briefings* are written by authorities who provide an effective, readable overview of their topics—not an academic monograph. The intended audience is busy nonspecialist readers who want to be informed concerning important issues in our industry in an accessible and timely manner.

Matthew Ismail, Editor in Chief

LIBRARY AS PUBLISHER

*New Models of Scholarly
Communication for a New Era*

SARAH KALIKMAN
LIPPINCOTT

Published in the United States of America by
ATG LLC (Media)
Manufactured in the United States of America

DOI: http://dx.doi.org/10.3998/mpub.9944345

ISBN 978-1-941269-16-9 (paper)
ISBN 978-1-941269-20-6 (e-book)

www.against-the-grain.com

CONTENTS

ACKNOWLEDGMENTS

I would like to thank Isaac Gilman, Holly Mercer, Charlotte Roh, David Seaman, and Allegra Swift for taking the time to share their insights, which greatly enriched this work. I am also grateful to Charles Watkinson for his thoughtful comments on the first draft of the manuscript.

INTRODUCTION

Over the last decade, in response to profound shifts in technology, policy, scholarly practices, and the marketplace, libraries have increasingly adopted the role of publisher. Academic libraries around the world are developing their own portfolios of journals, monographs, and conference proceedings and embracing less-traditional and less-formal types of publications, such as data sets, white papers, websites, and undergraduate scholarship. In 2001, Kate Wittenberg argued that this new landscape would require librarians and publishers to "rethink their modes of operation and their role in the cycle of creating and communicating knowledge" (p. 29). Libraries have largely heeded that call, distancing themselves from the role of information warehouse and devising new strategies that position them as active partners in the creation and dissemination of research.

Publishing has emerged as a natural outgrowth of and corollary to libraries' investment in scholarly communication, digital scholarship, and data management services, among others. Libraries, as information intermediaries, have a unique and advantageous position in this new "information environment" (Wittenberg, 2001, p. 29). They have an intimate knowledge of the information needs and practices of scholars on their campuses, a deep understanding of the scholarly publishing landscape across disciplines, and direct experience with the impact of new technology on both.

Though it has received increasing attention over the last several years, library publishing did not appear out of nowhere. As Okerson and Holzman (2015) note in their enlightening and comprehensive overview of the origins and foundations of library publishing, "Libraries have always published, mainly in modest ways and most often in particular niches (such as catalogs), producing some mighty results" (p. 2). They cite records of libraries publishing printed catalogs of their holdings as early as the 1600s and the fact that "certain major U.S. university presses [such as Cornell University Press] were started from within libraries" (p. 2). More recently, library-publisher collaborations such as Project Muse, Highwire Press, and Project Euclid, among other initiatives, launched in the early 1990s in response to escalating journal prices and the apparent need for innovation in scholarly publishing models (Thomas, 2006). In a 2001 article, Wittenberg described the Electronic Publishing Initiative at Columbia (EPIC) program at Columbia University, an early, formal library publishing effort that has many of the hallmarks of contemporary initiatives.

Over the past five years, however, library publishing has gained a critical mass within academic libraries and has garnered increasing attention from librarians and publishers alike. The Library Publishing Coalition (LPC), a membership association catering to the distinct needs of library publishers, counts more than 60 members globally and lists more than 115 libraries in its annual *Library Publishing Directory*. Meanwhile, a 2015 study determined that "one in four university libraries in Australia is publishing original scholarly works in some form (mostly journals)" (Missingham, 2015). Though library publishers still account for a small fraction of published scholarship, they are making notable contributions to the ecosystem. In 2016, for example, the academic libraries inventoried in the *Library Publishing Directory* published a total of 685 individual journal titles (excluding undergraduate research journals; LPC Directory Committee, 2016), compared with 1,160 individual journal titles published by American university presses (AAUP, 2016), and an estimated 25,000 total scholarly journal titles published annually (Esposito, 2013). Open access (OA) journal publishing is by far the most common activity for library publishers, but many libraries also boast active monograph publishing programs alongside considerable work in publishing gray literature, data, student work, and digital humanities projects.

As this variety of products indicates, library publishing is no mere scale replica of traditional scholarly publishing. Libraries have brought new models to the table—models inflected with the values and principles of academic librarianship, models designed to fill gaps in the publishing landscape, models designed to leverage the unique skills and positioning of libraries. The LPC identifies three core features that distinguish library publishing from related activities such as digitization programs and simple repository hosting. Library publishing "requires a production process, presents original work not previously made available, and applies a level of certification to the content published (whether through a peer review process or by extension of the library's institutional brand)" (LPC, 2016). A series of conference proceedings hosted exclusively and for the first time in the library's repository fits within these parameters. A library of digitized manuscripts does not. Though it may seem arbitrary, maintaining this distinction may help libraries to develop a unique and robust identity for their publishing program, which in turn builds the prestige and reputation that will attract authors and readers.

The fundamental model of library publishing is simple (Fig. 1). In the case of journal publishing, for instance, a faculty member may approach the library with her content, such as an idea for a new journal in her field of expertise. The faculty member provides the disciplinary expertise necessary to identify an audience for the content, to ensure a basic level of quality, and to build a pool of qualified peer reviewers and an editorial board. The librarian or librarians, in turn, provide the technology, skills, and infrastructure for production and dissemination, along with expertise in copyright and licensing, metadata, preservation, and other relevant topics. The library's existing institutional repository frequently serves as the publication's home.

Many library publishing initiatives may best be described as publishing *services* in that they put less emphasis on acquiring, managing, and owning a coherent portfolio of work and more on providing the necessary technologies

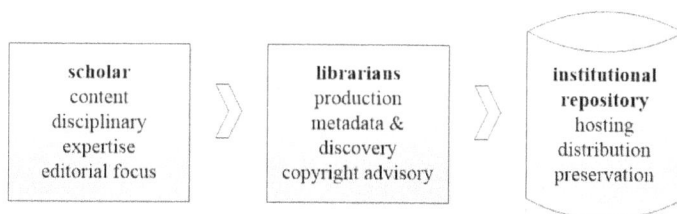

FIGURE 1. Library publishing service model

and support to facilitate content creation and dissemination of all kinds. The library commonly provides a suite of services related to the processes of production, hosting, and distribution, as well as training, guidance, and advising on technology, copyright, peer review, and other relevant topics. The precise roster of services varies widely, often depending on the skills and capacity of the library staff and the specific needs of the faculty and students who take advantage of the service. The most basic level of service requires only that the library make available a publishing platform, such as an institutional repository. However, most library publishers also provide copyright advisory, training (e.g., in the use of software), metadata creation and cataloging, digitization (e.g., for back issues of a journal), hosting of supplemental content (e.g., image collections), analytics (including altmetrics), outreach, and identifiers like ISSNs or DOIs.

Library publishers favor lightweight workflows, often both by preference and by necessity. They focus on digital publication, often dispensing with print entirely. Notably, libraries often eschew services that most other publishers consider integral parts of the enterprise, including notification of abstracting and indexing services, copyediting, typesetting, print on demand, and graphic design (LPC Directory Committee, 2016). It is this emphasis on lightweight, no-frills workflows that helps keep costs low and gives library publishers their characteristic agility. Digital-only or digital and print-on-demand publishing allows libraries to dispense with expensive print production and distribution services.

Frugal publishing does not mean free publishing, however. Like all publishers, libraries incur considerable costs, the most significant being staff time and the implementation and maintenance of a publishing platform. These costs are often covered through an institutional subsidy, usually from the library's operating budget—the pool of money that pays for library staffing, services, and spaces. Institutional subsidies allow libraries considerable freedom to experiment and to take on publications that are unwieldy or unprofitable. It also frees them from worrying about cost recovery. Unsurprisingly, library publishers exhibit an overwhelming preference for OA licensing, with more than 90 percent reporting that their portfolios are mostly or completely OA (Lippincott, 2014).

What forces have contributed to the remarkable proliferation of library publishing in recent years? Should all academic libraries follow suit? What considerations must they bear in mind? This book will introduce the reader to a variety of library-based publishing initiatives in the United States and Canada to address these and other important questions. Special attention will be paid to defining library publishing as a distinct and complementary sub-field of scholarly publishing, describing best practices and considerations for launching a publishing initiative in the library, and positing future directions for the library as publisher. The scope of this book is limited to academic libraries, although public libraries are also exploring new roles as publishers. It also pertains primarily to academic library publishing in North America and to a lesser extent the United Kingdom and Australia. Little published research exists, at least in English, on library publishing in other parts of the world, despite the growing popularity of OA journal publishing in the Global South. This book will be a valuable resource for librarians interested in launching or enhancing a publishing program; library administrators seeking to understand how publishing intersects with a variety of emerging library roles in data curation, digital humanities, OA, and faculty support; and scholarly publishers who want to learn more about how libraries are contributing to the publishing ecosystem.

WHY LIBRARY PUBLISHING?

In a post on library publishing for the influential *Scholarly Kitchen* blog, publishing consultant Joe Esposito (2013) asked rhetorically, "Why would anyone want to get into this business when those of us who were already there were trying desperately to get out?" The publishing community has established that publishing is not easy, it is not usually profitable at a small scale, it is in a constant state of "crisis," and it is dealing with a variety of challenges and tensions, from changes in technology to changes in the marketplace. So why don't libraries leave this up to the existing players? Charlotte Roh, scholarly communication librarian at the University of San Francisco, offers an explanation: Publishing is a natural fulfillment of librarians' role as information disseminators. Roh elaborates, "The easiest way to explain my job is to relate it to the traditional duty of librarians: making knowledge available now and for the future. Publishing is an extension of what a librarian has always done" (personal communication, January 30, 2017). Beyond its natural alignment with librarianship, the reasons for library publishing's growing popularity are manifold and nuanced. This section summarizes the major motivations behind this trend, from responding to frustrations with traditional scholarly publishing to showcasing libraries' unique collections.

OPENING ACCESS TO SCHOLARSHIP

The emergence of library publishing can be directly correlated with perceived failures of and inequities in the contemporary scholarly publishing ecosystem. As Thomas (2006) observed, "The disconnection between the producers of scholarly literature and the intermediaries who purchase it for consumption by others has generated a dysfunctional economic relationship" (p. 9). Scholarly, and especially scientific, publishing is increasingly dominated by a small number of large commercial publishers (Larivière, Haustein, & Mongeon, 2015). The costs of journal subscriptions, particularly for high-prestige science and engineering journals, have risen precipitously over the last couple of decades, squeezing library budgets and having a ripple effect on the broader scholarly publishing market. Libraries spend a greater share of their budgets on journal subscriptions, leaving less and less for monographs. University presses, which produce many of these monographs, especially in the humanities and social sciences, are being dually squeezed by shrinking subsidies from their parent institutions. Meanwhile, as commercial scholarly publishers begin to experiment with OA publication, libraries may also foot the bill for author fees or article processing charges (APCs).

"THE DISCONNECTION BETWEEN THE PRODUCERS OF SCHOLARLY LITERATURE AND THE INTERMEDIARIES WHO PURCHASE IT FOR CONSUMPTION BY OTHERS HAS GENERATED A DYSFUNCTIONAL ECONOMIC RELATIONSHIP."

In addition to escalating prices, librarians cite a number of other frustrations with the scholarly publishing marketplace. Commercial scholarly publishers typically protect their content with restrictive licenses and author agreements in conjunction with digital rights management (DRM) protections that aim to prevent unauthorized distribution or piracy. Authors retain limited rights to their work and limited control over how to distribute it. Scholars frequently experience long delays between submission and publication, potentially slowing the pace of innovation (Björk & Solomon, 2013). Scholars and librarians have also leveled substantial critiques against the traditional peer-review process, which may contribute to publication delays and has been accused of bias, ineffectiveness, and inconsistency (Smith, 2006). Commercial scholarly publishers have also been slow to integrate technologies that facilitate multimedia publication and place artificial limits on page numbers, figures, and other elements of a publication based on legacy print production requirements. Finally, commercial scholarly publishers and university presses have not provided solutions for publishing vast quantities of significant scholarship in the form of gray literature, data, learning objects, digital humanities projects, and other nontraditional forms of scholarly and creative output.

As these criticisms multiplied, librarians and others recognized opportunities, and even obligations, to address them. Many libraries have established OA publishing funds, contributed financially to a range of nonprofits dedicated to new publishing models, and created offices of scholarly communications and copyright to help authors on their campuses make informed publishing decisions. Library publishing is a natural outgrowth of this commitment to a more open and transparent scholarly communications environment.

Along with a commitment to more openness and transparency at the ecosystem level, libraries have seized opportunities to address local needs by working with faculty and students on their campuses. Where traditional publishers have left gaps or contributed to frustration, libraries see the potential for new services. Library publishers have actively addressed many faculty concerns, from restrictive licenses to long publication delays and limited support for new media. Specifically, library publishers provide alternative solutions for authors and editors looking for OA publication and permissive licensing.

OA advocates see an inherent conflict in commercial scholarly publishing. Faculty authors effectively give away their scholarship, produced with the resources made available by their institutions, to large corporations, who proceed to sell or lease it back to those same institutions at elevated prices. Scholars, librarians, funders, and other stakeholders have grown increasingly impatient with this model and have advanced a variety of alternative models to cover the costs of scholarly publishing while providing free and unhindered access to content. OA publishing in a variety of forms is garnering increasing support from faculty authors who are frustrated with the perceived inequities in commercial publishing and interested in ensuring that their work has the greatest possible impact and broadest possible reach. Studies have demonstrated a variety of advantages of OA publishing for authors, including increased citations (Wagner, 2010) and shorter delays between submission and publication (Van Noorden, 2013).

Libraries, which have long been at the forefront of OA advocacy, are increasingly investing in efforts that address these frustrations head on.

A growing number of start-ups and nonprofit initiatives, such as Knowledge Unlatched, Ubiquity Press, and the Open Library of the Humanities, are experimenting with models that fund the cost of publishing up front (through institutional/funder commitments, author fees, or a combination of the two) and make the end products freely and openly available. In addition to funding these and other initiatives, libraries also see a role for themselves in providing high-quality OA content and in empowering scholars to exert their influence in the publishing process. Giving authors control over their scholarship is a common promise from library publishers. The California Digital Library's eScholarship service prominently advertises that it "provides a suite of open access, scholarly publishing services and research tools that enable departments, research units, publishing programs, and individual scholars associated with the University of California to have direct control over the creation and dissemination of the full range of their scholarship" (University of California Office of Scholarly Communication, 2014).

In traditional publishing models, authors also cede much of the control over their scholarship through restrictive licenses that limit how authors can use and distribute their own work once it has been published. These licenses protect the publisher's investment in the content but can hinder access, especially to readers in developing nations or readers who have no academic affiliation. Restrictive licenses and digital rights management also prevent or impede activities like large-scale text mining of scholarly literature. Unlike commercial scholarly publishers, libraries "are based on a service model of sharing resources and free exchange . . . Library publishers are not gatekeepers; their mission is dissemination" (Royster, 2014, p. 96). As champions of dissemination, library publishers typically allow, encourage, or even require Creative Commons licenses for their publications. Permissive licensing practices facilitate the free and rapid flow of information and ensure that any interested reader can access content.

Libraries simultaneously facilitate informal publishing (such as collections of technical reports) and OA publishing that adheres to the highest scholarly standards. Scholarly publishers, researchers, and even librarians commonly repeat the misconception that library publications are not peer reviewed. In fact, Busher and Kamotsky (2016) found in a study of journals published on the Digital Commons platform that nearly all took advantage of the platform's built-in blind submission and peer-review features.

By supporting OA publication models and permissive licenses, library publishers are contributing to the volume of reputable, high-quality OA scholarship, providing models for sustainable OA publishing that can be adopted by other communities, and giving authors greater control over how their work is published and disseminated. Library publishing therefore provides an important alternative and complementary option to commercial scholarly publishing, an alternative that has growing appeal.

SUPPORTING NICHE AND EXPERIMENTAL PUBLICATIONS

Many library publishers have found a niche in catering to publications that break the mold. They embrace projects with limited readership and unconventional subjects and seek out high-quality content, regardless of its format or the logistical challenges of publication. Beginning in the early 2000s, libraries grasped the potential of institutional repositories to "apply serious, systematic leverage to accelerate changes taking place in scholarship and scholarly communication" (Lynch, 2003, p. 1). Early institutional and disciplinary repositories focused on faculty preprints and electronic theses and dissertations (ETDs) but increasingly showcase and steward a broad range of creative and intellectual outputs. Library publishing has enthusiastically taken up the charge of transforming scholarly communication by providing a home for the range of content that is routinely ignored by other scholarly publishers. Royster (2014) says of the University of Nebraska–Lincoln (UNL) library publishing program, "Our mission, as we see it, is to provide a publishing outlet for scholarly work that does not fit other available publication models, either because it is too long, too short, too esoteric, too expensive, too complicated, or just too strange" (p. 100).

Work that "does not fit" often includes journals and monographs on niche or interdisciplinary topics; gray literature (e.g., preprints, dissertations, conference proceedings, white papers, and technical reports); and newer forms of research output that often go unpublished (e.g., research data, digital humanities projects, websites, teaching materials, audiovisual materials, maps, and three-dimensional models). Although articles and monographs remain the primary vehicles of scholarly communication, scholars increasingly rely on this broad array of other formal and informal publications to advance discourse in their fields. Historically, these nontraditional products of academic research lacked proper dissemination channels, despite their academic merit and potential readership. Libraries found them challenging to obtain and make available to readers. Library publishers increasingly provide a stable, citable, and discoverable home that ensures that these important research outputs do not disappear from the scholarly record. The Purdue University Libraries, for example, publishes a highly consulted series of technical reports in partnership with the Joint Transportation Research Program. The reports in the series, which have been downloaded more than 400,000 times, represent "a treasure trove of invaluable information for transportation professionals" (Newton, Bullock, Watkinson, Bracke, & Horton, 2011). ArXiv, a preprint server for physics and related disciplines administered and partially funded by the Cornell University Library (https://arxiv .org/), has become one of the most prominent and well-used collections of gray literature.

At the other end of the spectrum from gray literature and other informal publications, libraries have also embraced experimental, multimedia publications and digital humanities projects. For these custom, often highly technical projects, libraries see an advantage in being small and entrepreneurial. Large commercial publishers benefit from economies of scale, but large publishing portfolios can also necessitate standardization and a lack of flexibility. Libraries, without the pressures of generating revenue or increasing efficiency, may be more open to customizing many aspects of a publication, from its policies to the look and feel of its templates, based on the wishes of authors and editors. Harriett Green of the University of Illinois at Urbana-Champaign (UIUC), who previously worked in university press publishing, observes that library publishing "allows for flexible, non-traditional formats and is much more lightweight. Some might call it bare bones, but I think it's much more agile" (personal communication, January 31, 2017). Authors and editors, she says, benefit from increased transparency and more input throughout the publishing process. Libraries can also take on multimedia projects that require sophisticated technology and a willingness to experiment. The Emory

University Libraries, for example, have long published a pioneering multimedia journal, *Southern Spaces* (https://southernspaces.org/), which takes full advantage of the digital medium. Other notable examples of multimedia publications include *Public* (http://public.imaginingamerica.org/welcome/), a multimedia journal published by Syracuse University Libraries, and *The Joy of Sanskrit* (http://press.anu.edu.au/titles/anu-etext/the-joy-of-sanskrit), a multimedia textbook published by the Australian National University. Digital humanities projects can, however, become liabilities. They require substantial initial investment and significant ongoing maintenance and updating. Their impact may be limited both by libraries' marketing capacity and by technological challenges to the long-term viability of complex digital objects. Vinopal and McCormick (2013) provide excellent guidance on how libraries can position services and triage digital publishing projects to help maximize impact and build a sustainable portfolio.

Libraries' tolerance for experimentation means that new projects can be launched without intensive assessment and planning. New publications can get off the ground with minimal lead time and evolve over time in response to successes and failures. As Charlotte Roh of the University of San Francisco observes, "The great thing about library publishing is that it's such a flexible endeavor. You can start a new journal without considering whether there's a market for it. If a faculty member proposes publishing a journal on human rights, we can take on the project just because we know the topic is important" (personal communication, February 1, 2017). Green, English and digital humanities librarian at UIUC, underscores the value of providing faculty with "opportunities for rapid, dynamic publishing that supports the evolving ways that scholars communicate within and across disciplines" (personal communication, January 31, 2017).

Libraries have also found a niche supporting journals and monographs on esoteric topics with extremely limited audiences. Though their readership may be small, these publications often represent the foremost (or only) venues for scholarship in their niche. Ohio State University's *International Journal of Screendance* (http://screendancejournal.org/), for example, purports to be "the first-ever scholarly journal wholly dedicated to this growing area of worldwide interdisciplinary practice." Despite its particularly narrow focus, the *Journal of Muslim Mental Health* (http://www.journalofmuslimmentalhealth.org/), published by Michigan Publishing Services, is an important and well-respected publication whose articles routinely receive high altmetrics scores. Libraries also embrace interdisciplinary publications, such as Penn State University's *Indigenous Knowledge: Other Ways of Knowing* (https://journals.psu.edu/ik) or the University of Windsor's *Informal Logic* (http://informallogic.ca/), which may not fit neatly into traditional publishers' editorial programs.

In 2011, October Ivins and Judy Luther elaborated a proposal for the libraries of large research universities to adopt small society publications, which were, especially at the time, often print only and struggling to maintain a financial foothold. Though the authors found that there was rarely a one-to-one match between libraries with the capacity to publish and society journals with some affiliation with the campus, the idea remains promising. Jones (2014) observes that "librarian publishers have already begun to make a positive difference in the publishing landscape by rescuing small, print-only journals from historical oblivion and providing the technical support and platform services to get them online and more importantly, discoverable." Library publishing services for these types of journals may include digitization of the publication's backfiles as well as the development and maintenance of the journal website. Libraries often provide extensive support to journal editors by offering training in using publishing platforms, guidance on policy and legal issues, and support for publishing workflows.

Royster (2014) offers two compelling examples of how libraries can provide a home for high-quality scholarly work that goes unpublished for financial and logistical reasons and not based on its scholarly merit or potential impact. In Royster's first example, a dictionary of invertebrate zoology authored by a faculty member at UNL was accepted for publication and had undergone peer review at a university press only to be dropped when the publisher "decided to get out of zoology publishing" (2014, p. 99). Two other scholarly publishers declined to publish the work for logistical reasons before it was ultimately published by UNL's library publishing imprint, Zea Books. Royster also details the struggle of an anthology of essays and illustrations relating to Hopi art, culture, and history, also ultimately published by UNL. Royster (2014) explains that the book's 75 color illustrations deterred commercial publishers, while "digital production made it possible for [Zea Books] to do the work as both an ebook and a print-on-demand hardcover"

(p. 99). These and other peer-reviewed, high-quality publications may not be profitable or marketable through traditional channels but nevertheless warrant dissemination. Libraries can decide to take on these projects based exclusively on their merits rather than on market forces.

ALIGNING WITH LIBRARY SERVICES AND VALUES

Publishing can fit well within an existing portfolio of library activities as disparate as data curation and undergraduate information literacy, institutional repository programs, and digital scholarship centers. It also aligns with libraries' commitment to equity and access. New modes of scholarship and new communication channels have blurred the lines between formal and informal scholarly communication (Brown, Griffiths, Rascoff, & Guthrie, 2007) and have disrupted our very notions of publication. Perhaps the clearest connections can be drawn between library publishing and other library services aimed at creating and stewarding digital content, such as data curation services and digital scholarship centers. Journal publishing programs fit neatly alongside many libraries' existing investments in data publishing services. Data and journal publishing can often be accommodated through the same publishing platform, and workflows and vendor relationships (such as those required for DOI minting) apply in both cases. Digital scholarship units can also productively complement library publishing programs, as both types of services engage librarians and faculty as partners in the creation and dissemination of scholarship. Both publishing and digital scholarship support require coding and design staff and robust content management and web publishing expertise. Staff with experience in scholarly journal and monograph publishing may also be helpful in supporting the vetting, review, and preservation of digital scholarship.

As data curation, digital scholarship programs, special collections digitization programs, and other emerging services demonstrate, libraries see highlighting and stewarding unique content as increasingly strategic. Redirecting resources from collecting to producing content is a natural response to information ubiquity (Gilman, 2015). Building vast collections of print and electronic resources has grown less strategic in a networked environment, in which libraries routinely share resources within consortia and around the world. This same environment allows libraries to showcase and disseminate the unique content their campuses produce and collect, from digitized manuscripts to faculty working papers. Holly Mercer of the University of Tennessee Libraries believes many untapped possibilities for library publishers remain, even within their walls. She proposes that libraries "look inward to our special collections and see what's there that might make publications that have broad interest" (personal communication, January 30, 2017). Thomas (2006) describes a vision in which libraries host "interconnected centers of excellence that link scholarship in various subject domains: labor history, nanofabrication, Islamic studies, philosophy, and others," building on the individual research strengths of their institutions (p. 10).

Publishing programs can align equally well with libraries' teaching and learning missions. Open Educational Resource (OER) or open textbook publishing engages libraries directly in the process of ensuring that all students have access to high-quality learning materials. The Open SUNY Textbooks program, for example, funds the publication of a series of textbooks published by State University of New York faculty for high-enrollment classes in the SUNY system. Oregon State University (OSU) Libraries launched a similar program in 2013 that provided a $15,000 stipend to OSU faculty (via a budget transfer) to produce an open textbook. The competitive application process emphasized the "use of extensive, original multimedia and interactive content" (Sutton & Chadwell, 2014, p. 41).

In addition to publishing content aimed at an undergraduate audience, libraries are also helping their students gain a deeper understanding of scholarly communication as an integral part of the academic endeavor. Duckett and Warren (2013) argue, "If librarians are to help students become information literate within an academic context—one in which they must find, understand, and use scholarly sources—teaching students about how scholars communicate seems like a pretty fundamental undertaking" (p. 26). By incorporating scholarly communication literacy into instruction sessions, librarians help students become savvier information consumers and producers.

Some libraries are taking this approach a step further by engaging their students in the publishing process as editors and producers of undergraduate research journals. This hands-on approach can help undergraduates develop a deeper understanding of how scholarship is created and disseminated and illustrate the abstract concepts that librarians already teach in information literacy sessions. Supporting undergraduate research journals entails an ongoing and intensive commitment to combat the constant turnover inherent in any student-run activity. Weiner and Watkinson (2014) found, in an examination of undergraduate research journals inventoried on the website of the Council for Undergraduate Research, that "a consistent feature of the journals that were struggling was that they appeared to be entirely student run, with the inevitable problems of staff turnover, while successful and sustainable publications always had a permanent home within the institution" (p. 3). Libraries can provide the stability and mentoring needed to run student research journals that showcase undergraduate scholarship and build information literacy and other relevant skills.

Indeed, library publishing leverages many of libraries' existing strengths, including instruction and advisory roles, organization of information, knowledge of the scholarly publishing landscape, and access to and discovery of resources. Many of the skills librarians cultivate are transferable between traditional library responsibilities and publishing activities. Thomas (2006) specifically identifies librarians' "knowledge of information management, organization, and sources" (p. 10). She observes, "With their experience in the digital domain and their familiarity with a broad spectrum of the end products of research, scholarly publications, they are well placed to facilitate innovative models of scholarly communication" (p. 10).

Robertson and Simser (2013) describe how the skills they developed as serials librarians inform their current roles, which have increasingly transitioned to support their libraries' publishing programs. They cite a strong "understanding [of] the role of serials, articles and monographs in scholarly publishing; familiarity with standards (existing and developing); familiarity with technology including work on administrative clients of the ILS [integrated library system] or using a variety of vendor platforms to manage e-journal knowledge bases or to customize database front ends for users; organizational skills and attention to details; familiarity with issues related to scholarly communication, open access and licensing; [and] experience working with vendors" (p. 126).

Relationships, like skills, can also be transferable. Charlotte Roh at the University of San Francisco says that faculty partners value the "library's connection with lots of parts of campus, in both research and administration, which offer connections to resources beyond their department" (personal communication, February 1, 2017). Green at UIUC also found that existing relationships with faculty, cultivated as a departmental liaison, translated into trust and an interest in deeper partnerships. Green found that despite having worked in publishing before going into libraries, she relies heavily on the soft skills she has developed as a librarian. In particular, she cites librarians' experience with "working with patrons to guide them to information they need" as critical to her work building author-driven publications (personal communication, January 30, 2017).

Finally, library publishers have also increasingly recognized an opportunity to address systemic inequities in scholarly publishing by explicitly adopting social justice values and actively publishing work by and about underrepresented groups. This philosophy aligns well with libraries' commitment to the public good and to promoting the creation and discovery of knowledge. Roh (2016) challenges the library profession to ask itself, "Are we perpetuating the biases and power structures of traditional scholarly publishing? Or are we using library publishing to interrogate, educate, and establish more equitable models of scholarly communication?" Library publishers who have made social justice a part of their mission will encourage their journal editors to examine the demographics of their editorial boards, the scholars who submit articles to their publication, and those whose work is ultimately published. Failing to address systemic inequities harms both "the authors who are not being published and therefore do not achieve tenure and promotion, and . . . the researchers who do not have access to the full range of possible scholarship" (Roh, 2016).

LIBRARIES ENJOY A UNIQUE AND ADVANTAGEOUS POSITION ON THEIR CAMPUSES THAT MAKES THEM PARTICULARLY WELL SUITED FOR SCHOLARLY PUBLISHING.

Libraries enjoy a unique and advantageous position on their campuses that makes them particularly well suited for scholarly publishing. They cultivate deep connections across campus with faculty, students, research centers, and other units and have experience working in partnership with their constituents. They have extensive knowledge of the processes and products of scholarly communication and have experience managing content, from vendor-supplied print and electronic collections to the original content in their institutional repositories. Libraries' service orientation, their commitment to supporting the research and teaching missions of their universities, may represent their greatest asset. As service providers, libraries are constantly evolving and experimenting to meet their constituents' needs and have their fingers on the pulse of the academy.

STARTING OR GROWING
A PUBLISHING PROGRAM
Considerations and Recommendations

This section offers a quick-start guide to library publishing, including recommendations for gaining traction for your initiative, selecting appropriate technologies, developing thoughtful policies and procedures, and developing organizational and business models that position you for success. The underlying theme of this section is the need for each library publisher to clearly and thoroughly define its mission and objectives. As Karla Hahn noted in 2008, "Library-based publishing programs are pragmatic responses to evident needs, not services in search of clients" (p. 24). Thoughtful evaluation of campus needs is a critical first step in building a successful service that is tailored to the institutional context. A publishing program optimized for publishing undergraduate journals may look very different from one designed primarily to publish scholarly monographs. It is clear from the variety of emerging models and the seemingly infinite permutations of services, business models, staffing, and policies, that a one-size-fits-all approach will not work for library publishing. Library publishing is, by definition, experimental. It is also deeply sensitive to the needs of its stakeholders, which vary significantly depending on the institutional context. The following recommendations are therefore intended to provide general guidance on the considerations any would-be library publisher should bear in mind and are not meant as a road map for implementation. Each section below incorporates advice and perspective from practicing library publishers and concludes with a brief list of further readings and resources relevant to each topic.

DEFINING YOUR NICHE

Publishing is never an end unto itself. Authors create their work with the expectation that it will be read. Publishers acquire and disseminate content with the expectation that it will find an interested audience, and they make every effort to ensure that it does. For libraries aspiring to launch publishing programs, defining internal and external audiences is therefore an essential first step. Internal audiences include the faculty and students who produce publishable scholarly and creative works. External audiences are the groups of readers, no matter how small, who would find these works of interest. Why would an author publish with your library? Why and how will a reader connect with your publication?

In order to attract high-quality publications and build a robust market for their services, library publishers must define their unique value proposition. Commercial and mission-driven scholarly publishers, such as university presses and scholarly societies, offer prestige, visibility, and professional support for their authors. Authors have confidence that these publishers will give their work a broad reach, a high impact, and a polished look. The most sophisticated library publishers can offer these benefits, but many libraries have more modest service offerings and limited reach. However, library publishers can also offer unique advantages. They generally boast the least restrictive licenses, embrace experimental publications, and offer unparalleled flexibility and a service orientation. Green, English and digital humanities librarian at the UIUC, considers flexibility their greatest asset. According to Green, "Our authors see a lot more behind the scenes and have more input throughout the process. Because our publishing program is nascent, our authors have a real chance to shape our workflows and how we work with them. We are truly author-driven" (personal communication, January 30, 2017).

Institutional subsidies contribute to libraries' flexibility and tolerance for experimentation. Holly Mercer, associate dean of research and scholarly communication at the University of Tennessee, explains, "We're not trying to make money or even break even, so we can consider supporting authors and publications that might not find the right supporters or right venue otherwise. If it's something that's good scholarship with a niche audience, a small number of readers that will benefit, that's good enough" (personal communication, January 30, 2017). Whether or not they follow the same selection criteria as other scholarly publishers, library publishers should be able to justify investing resources in a publication. Fundamentally, libraries should be able to identify a potential audience, even an extremely small one, for each publication they take on. Identifying potential audiences helps libraries avoid the appearance of so-called vanity publishing and forms the basis of marketing efforts. Identifying audiences and impact goals in advance also helps library publishers measure which publications have been successful, informing their future projects. Isaac Gilman, university librarian and library director at Pacific University, encourages librarians to establish a solid rationale for a publishing program and each publication in their portfolio. He explains that librarians should ask themselves whether they are "developing a publishing service that meets an external need; that you're not publishing into the void for the sake of offering a service" (personal communication, January 30, 2017).

Though lightweight workflows are one of the hallmarks of library publishing, libraries should thoughtfully consider which aspects of traditional publishing they adopt and which they discard. What may at first appear lightweight can easily become haphazard. David Seaman of the Syracuse University Libraries cautions that libraries easily neglect the fundamental processes that make publishing successful. He explains, "Left to our own devices, what libraries do tends not to look like publishing. We tend not to do marketing or design. Library publications are often substandard in their design and [have] no sense of active promotion. We should take a moment to understand what are the skills that make up publishing, beyond the mechanics of dissemination" (personal communication, February 17, 2017).

The library's publishing niche will also be heavily informed by "what is already available or what is missing in their institutional environment, such as a university press or another department with overlapping interests" (Ivins & Luther, 2011, p. 13). Conversations with potential partners and complementary service providers can provide valuable contextual information and help form connections that can be deepened over time.

Recommended Reading and Resources

- Royster (2014) describes the process of building a coherent publishing portfolio at the UNL Libraries. His case study provides a thoughtful examination of how a library publisher can infuse its program with library values and play to the campus's strengths.
- Richard Carlin (2016), executive editor at Oxford University Press, gives a useful overview of the process of building a list in an article for *Against the Grain*.
- Vinopal's (2012) article on project portfolio management offers an excellent framework for thinking programmatically about publishing rather than focusing solely on individual publications.

BUILDING SUPPORT

Library publishing initiatives often emerge organically as a result of unmet needs. The level and flavor of these needs will vary by institution, making needs assessment a crucial first step in establishing a publishing program. Gilman urges librarians to "make sure there's someone other than you in your community who wants this to happen. There's something to be said for being a visionary and being out in front, but I think it would be hard to build a publishing service if there wasn't some recognition from within your community that it was valuable or necessary" (Gilman, personal communication, January 30, 2017). Thoughtful environmental scanning, needs assessment, and advocacy can supplement anecdotal observations and individual requests for support and help establish a solid footing for growing a full-fledged publishing initiative. This section provides brief guidance on the first steps to launching a library publishing program that is informed by and responds to constituent needs.

UNDERTAKE A CAMPUS PUBLISHING AUDIT. Libraries may be surprised to find that journal publishing is already under way on their campus, whether it's the passion projects of individual faculty members or student organizations or the products of research institutes, centers, and departments. An inventory of the publications that could benefit from a centralized, professional publishing partner can be a convincing tool when advocating for resources. It also helps you identify those partners on campus who might be most eager to work with your library. Productive approaches to identifying faculty publications include perusing faculty and departmental web pages, conducting a web survey, and working directly with liaison librarians, who often have intimate knowledge of their faculty's research.

If the results of this audit reveal little publishing activity or a lack of obvious interest, Green, the UIUC librarian, advises taking a slower route, such as "supporting basic instruction and training related to publishing, providing hosting through Omeka, Scalar, and other basic platforms, rather than becoming a full-fledged publisher" (personal communication, January 31, 2017). UIUC elected to take this slower route, gradually establishing the library as a resource. Over time, they saw interest in publishing with the library blossom, and "now people are coming out of the woodwork." This process can also establish the library as a trusted resource for author and editor advising services, from helping scholars negotiate author agreements to referring aspiring journal editors to external publishing services. Green observes, "Even if you're not publishing on your campus, sometimes what students and faculty need is guidance. Build up the knowledge and capacity to advise on scholarly communication and OA issues or offer referral services to other library publishers who are willing to work with external authors" (personal communication, January 31, 2017).

TALK TO FACULTY (AND STUDENTS) ABOUT THEIR PUBLISH-ING NEEDS AND PAIN POINTS. A robust needs assessment may also include a survey of or interviews with faculty and students to better understand their needs. These conversations help establish a rationale for the university to support publishing and may help library publishers identify the specific particular services, tools, or platforms they should support. Citing specific, documented needs from faculty and students can be a powerful advocacy tool. Decision makers who may be reluctant to invest in a new, experimental service may be swayed by evidence of its potential impact. David Seaman, dean of libraries at Syracuse University, observes, "You tend to get better results when you have a clear, thoughtful statement of what success looks like. If you're looking to sway your administration, faculty and student voices count for a lot. If you can demonstrate that their scholarship would be greatly enhanced if you could publish their data sets, that can be a convincing argument" (personal communication, February 17, 2017).

RUN A PILOT. Developing a publishing program cannot occur in a vacuum. It is difficult to anticipate every necessary resource, develop comprehensive policies, and gain experience without concrete projects to put your ideas to the test. Pilot projects "provide the groundwork to define a publishing service strategy . . . answering the questions of how the library can publish original materials and later on assessing next steps" (Furlough, 2011, p. 14). In many cases, pilot projects come in the form of faculty or student requests for support. David Seaman of the Syracuse University Libraries recommends this learning-by-doing approach for libraries building a publishing program. He advises selecting pilot projects that "get you thinking about what publishing means in a practical way and move you beyond the logistics of making something digital and sticking it on the web." When expectations are clearly defined, these endeavors represent a learning opportunity for the library and the author or editor and may result in a publication that makes all parties proud. Ideal pilot projects, according to Seaman, have a manageable scope and level of commitment. They are also inexpensive. Seaman notes, "If you can do the project on your own dime, it's not held hostage by needing a grant or three new positions to achieve success" (personal communication, February 17, 2017).

SCALE UP. Libraries typically adopt a staged approach to building their program rather than launching a full-fledged publishing initiative all at once. The Pacific University Libraries, for example, began experimenting with one-off projects six years ago and "added publications organically as opportunities arose" (Gilman, personal communication, January 30, 2017). During this start-up phase, the library did not request direct financial support, only the staff time needed to run these ad hoc ventures. Gilman notes that this approach gave the library an "opportunity to prove ourselves and the value of what we were doing" (personal communication, January 30, 2017). Once they could demonstrate the value of the initiative, the library had a strong case for additional support to build on its success. At the end of this process, Pacific University found its administration receptive. Administrators, Gilman says, saw the opportunity to "extend the brand and impact of the institution in core areas" through a publishing program and were interested in supporting the common good through OA publishing. They also saw the potential value of providing students and faculty with opportunities to participate in scholarly communication.

In order to scale up, library publishers need to build both capacity and demand. Increasing capacity may require new staffing lines or reallocated staff time or additional funding to hire vendors and freelancers to do work that cannot be completed in house. Building demand for services does not mean manufacturing a need; rather, it means conducting campus outreach, cultivating an image as a trustworthy and reputable partner, and demonstrating the impact of your work. Finally, scaling up involves taking a hard look at the direct and indirect costs of publishing and assessing the value of your publishing program as it relates to the institutional mission, the library's strategic goals, and the success of faculty and students. Costs and business models are discussed in more detail in a subsequent section.

Recommended Reading and Resources

- LaRose and Kahn (2016) describe the process of conducting a "comprehensive survey of publishing activity" at the University of Michigan.
- Furlough (2011) provides a narrative account of four library publishing programs' start-up phases, which may provide a useful template for other libraries.
- Welzenbach and Colman (2015) describe the process of scaling up at Michigan Publishing Services by implementing fee-based publishing services.
- Werner (2015) describes a so-called incubator model for journal publishing that allowed the University of Utrecht library to scale up its OA publishing operation.

PLATFORMS AND TECHNOLOGY

The most widely implemented library publishing platforms include bepress's Digital Commons and the Public Knowledge Project's (PKP) family of software, including Open Journal Systems (OJS), Open Conference Systems (OCS), and Open Monograph Publishing (OMP). Libraries also employ a range of other purpose-built, customized, and homegrown applications. Modern publishing platforms typically facilitate a variety of publishing processes, including manuscript submission, peer review, editing, XML markup, format conversion, and content hosting, either through built-in functionality or through integration with third-party applications or plug-ins.

The choice of publishing platform may be informed by the infrastructure already in place—for example, if your library already maintains an institutional repository platform that can accommodate publishing workflows. Libraries face a fundamental choice between open source systems that must be installed and maintained on library servers and proprietary software maintained and administered by a third-party service provider. Open source platforms offer excellent flexibility, extensibility, and interoperability and are friendly to a wide variety of media (Corbett, Ghaphery, Work, & Byrd, 2016). However, they also require significant technical expertise to install, customize, and maintain. Hosted solutions offer rapid implementation and robust technical support and training supplied by the vendor. On the other hand, they entail significant ongoing costs and offer limited options for customization. Several of the most popular publishing platforms are briefly profiled below. Each platform has its own advantages and shortcomings. Selecting a publishing platform ultimately rests on your library's philosophy, technical infrastructure and staffing, and desired functionality.

BEPRESS DIGITAL COMMONS. Originally designed as an institutional repository platform, Digital Commons has gained increasing popularity as a journal publishing platform. It is the most popular publishing platform among libraries (LPC Directory Committee, 2016). As a hosted platform, Digital Commons offers limited flexibility and options for customization. It is optimized for PDF and other file hosting and would not be a robust choice for library publishers who wish to focus on multimedia publications or new media. Despite these drawbacks, Digital Commons is fully hosted, well supported, and frequently updated based on user community feedback.

OPEN JOURNAL SYSTEMS (OJS). The second most popular publishing platform among libraries (LPC Directory Committee, 2016), OJS provides a straightforward, open source solution for e-journal publishing. It supports editorial and production workflows and can be customized with a journal's branding and other display preferences. The basic publication homepages are fairly simple but can be easily customized with the journal's branding. For an example of a basic journal setup, see the *McGill Journal of Education* (http://mje.mcgill.ca/). More sophisticated customization is possible, as evidenced by PLAID (http://theplaidjournal.com/), a project of the Florida State University College of Medicine and the Charlotte Edwards Maguire Medical Library. OJS is optimized for PDF and HTML content but does support integration of images and media.

DSPACE. Many libraries employ DSpace, developed by Cornell University, as an institutional repository solution. Like all open source software, DSpace requires significant up-front investment in installation as well as ongoing maintenance by library staff. While it provides robust content organization and hosting, it lacks support for workflows such as manuscript submission and review and format conversion and therefore may not be ideal for libraries that intend to undertake journal and monograph publishing.

WORDPRESS. Ambitious library publishers with considerable technical expertise or a budget for development may consider customizing WordPress as a publishing platform. The library-published journal *Southern Spaces* (https://southernspaces.org/) transitioned in 2016 from Drupal to WordPress and remains an exemplary demonstration of the potential of a content management system to publish dynamic, multimedia content. WordPress can also facilitate monograph publishing via the PressBooks plug-in, which creates publication-ready print-on-demand and e-book files.

DRUPAL. Like WordPress, Drupal is a content management system. It is open source and highly flexible and offers extremely powerful tools for dynamic display of content. It is supported by an active developer community and an array of well-documented modules that can work together to create a robust publishing platform. E-Journal, a module designed specifically for journal publishing, is no longer supported but demonstrates the aptitude of Drupal as a journal publishing platform. McHale (2011) cites Drupal's flexibility, its powerful content management functionality, and the array of customizable modules as its primary advantages. However, the steep learning curve and the technical expertise required for the initial installation and configuration may deter many libraries from adopting this system.

FULL-SERVICE SOLUTIONS. A variety of new start-ups are offering publishing platforms and services designed specifically for OA and university-based publishing. Ubiquity Press was founded as an OA publisher in 2012. In addition to publishing its own content, it also offers its publishing platform to its network of partner presses. The University of Cologne's Modern Academic Publishing (MAP) service, for example, utilizes the platform for their open monograph series (http://www.humanities-map.net/). Ubiquity Press's platform offers a more modern in-browser reading experience than many of its competitors and supports a full range of editorial and production workflows. The full-service journal publishing start-up Scholastica has found a growing niche with academic law reviews like the *Arizona State Law Journal* (http://arizonastatelawjournal.org/). Reasonable author fees fund the service, which offers an excellent manuscript submission and peer-review interface as well as a journal hosting service. Scholastica is a compelling option for libraries that choose not to host journals themselves.

NEXT-GENERATION DIGITAL PUBLISHING. In addition to the many robust solutions for journal and monograph publishing, a fleet of emerging open source platforms explores the connections between publishing and digital humanities, following in the tradition of pioneering digital storytelling platform Scalar (http://scalar.usc.edu/). Notable examples include Vega, a forthcoming multimedia publishing platform being developed by Cheryl Ball and colleagues at West Virginia University (http://vegapublish.com/); Manifold, a new digital monograph publishing platform from the University of Minnesota Press (http://manifold.umn.edu/); and Fulcrum, a platform under development at the University of Michigan that will allow flexible digital publishing and robust integration of digital objects (https://www.fulcrum.org/).

Recommended Reading and Resources

- Though some of the technical specifics may be out of date, the *Columbia Guide to Digital Publishing* (Kasdorf, 2003) provides a comprehensive and detailed primer on digital publishing technology, addressing topics such as XML markup, metadata, document structure, and more.

- Publishing start-up Scholastica has produced a helpful guide to the mechanics of digital journal publishing, including topics such as developing a journal's web presence, format considerations (PDF, HTML, or both), and tips for enhancing search engine discovery of the journal's content (https://scholasticahq.com/definitive-guide-to-journal -publishing).

ORGANIZATION, STAFFING, AND PARTNERSHIPS

Library publishing programs frequently take advantage of existing technological and human resources. Many begin as low-investment experiments that use the library's institutional repository—which often already hosts faculty preprints, ETDs, and other content—to host more formal publications such as e-journals and monographs. As early as 2007, Paul Royster at UNL noted the disproportionate popularity of the *original* content archived in the library's institutional repository. "This suggests," Royster (2007) concluded, "a role for the IRs [institutional repositories] beyond that of archival storage and accessibility enhancement: in fact, they are well suited to become online publishers giving voice to a wide range of authors normally excluded, put off, or ill-served by the vagaries, idiosyncrasies, delays, obligations, and hoops-jumping of the conventional publication routes" (p. 2).

The range of units and departments in which publishing takes place (including Scholarly Communications, Digital Initiatives, and Library Technology) indicates the experimental and highly context-dependent nature of publishing in libraries. Other libraries have a dedicated Digital Publishing, Digital Scholarship, or Publishing and Data Services unit (LPC Directory Committee, 2016). In some cases, the library establishes an imprint or a full-fledged press to carry out its publishing ambitions. The United Kingdom, Germany, and Australia in particular have witnessed the revitalization of university presses as an integral part of the university library. This phenomenon is less common, though not unheard of, in the United States. Other presses that have been newly founded by libraries include the Amherst College Press and the Lever Press initiative. Other libraries have established imprints, such as Zea E-Books at UNL, or more commonly, an existing press has been reorganized as part of the library, as in the case of Purdue University Libraries and Press. As of 2016, nearly 30 percent of university presses in the United States reported to a library (Watkinson, 2016). In some cases, this manifests as a purely administrative relationship; in others, active collaboration and cooperation have been fostered (Lippincott, 2016; Watkinson, 2016).

Staffing for library publishing programs is lean and often relies on reallocated staff time rather than new, dedicated positions. Libraries report an average of around two full-time equivalents in professional staffing (LPC Directory Committee, 2016). Many libraries supplement their staffing with paraprofessional staff and with graduate and undergraduate student assistants and may outsource some work to freelancers or vendors. Library publishers may find it challenging to find vendors who will take on clients with such small portfolios, but a growing number of services are recognizing libraries as potential customers for publication management systems, conversion services, and copyediting, among other tools and services.

Though library publishing staffing is often lean, a large, formal initiative will require more than a skeleton crew. Roh observes, "Libraries want to hire one person to do all these roles that in the publishing world require a team of people. The result is that work gets distributed back to authors and editors. Managing that is something I had to learn" (personal communication, February 1, 2017). Libraries that wish to produce professional-looking publications and build high-impact portfolios of content may need additional positions related to graphic design and typesetting, marketing and outreach, acquisition and editing, and coding and web design. Creating professional-looking content—publications that are well designed, copyedited, and readable—is essential, says David Seaman of Syracuse University Libraries. He notes, "Production values are important in any industry; a badly put together page reflects on the content" (personal communication, February 17, 2017). Skinner, Lippincott, Speer, and Walters (2014) recommend cultivating and hiring for soft skills such as relationship management, openness to experimentation, and a keen grasp of scholarship, as many of the more technical skills such as layout and copyediting can be increasingly outsourced or automated. They also advise that publishers will increasingly rely on staff with strong technology skills as dynamic, multimedia publications gain in popularity.

To compensate for skills, time, and expertise their staff may lack, library publishers take advantage of their relationships with a range of campus partners. At UIUC, Green works regularly with the copyright unit, the institutional repository, metadata librarians, instruction librarians, the research data services unit, and the campus's digital scholarship center (personal communication, January 31, 2017). A partnership with the university press can be particularly valuable for libraries with the luxury of having one on their campus. Seaman observes, "Librarians often have the technical skills and equipment to publish, but we generally lack staff with any direct experience in academic publishing. We lack the industry sense of what it means to publish from the insider's perspective" (personal communication, February 17, 2017). University press and library collaborations have garnered increasing attention recently, especially as a growing number of presses now report to their library. Seaman advises taking full advantage of their expertise and perspective. He explains, "Having a relationship with the press doesn't mean you have to emulate them entirely. We may not be looking to sell content, but we're certainly looking for it to be discovered, reviewed, impactful, and reflect well on the institution, which is also what [the] press wants" (personal communication, February 17, 2017).

> CREATING PROFESSIONAL-LOOKING CONTENT . . . IS ESSENTIAL.

Recommended Reading and Resources

- The Library Publishing Coalition (LPC) maintains a job board (https://librarypublishing.org/resources/jobs) where library publishers can post openings or glean ideas about the types of positions they might need and the skills and qualifications they require.
- The LPC also maintains an inventory of professional development, training, and certification opportunities for library publishers at http://librarypublishing.org/resources/professionaldevelopment.

- Furlough (2011) provides a thoughtful analysis of the skills library publishers must cultivate in a variety of areas, including strategy development, content production and management, and distribution and marketing. Librarians may find particularly enlightening Furlough's discussion of how nascent publishing programs can reallocate staffing to support start-up efforts.
- Skinner, Lippincott, Speer, and Walters (2014) forecast the skills and training that will be required of the next generation of publishing professionals.
- Watkinson (2016) and Roh (2014) provide compelling state-of-the-field reports and explorations of the advantages of library and university press collaboration.

POLICIES AND PROCEDURES

Though it may be impossible to plan for every eventuality, savvy library publishers understand that developing thoughtful, university-counsel-vetted policies, contracts, and documentation saves time and prevents headaches. Publishing programs require high-level policies that address both what kinds of authors the library will work with and the services they will provide, as well as publication-specific contracts or memoranda of understanding that specifically elaborate the rights and responsibilities of the publisher and author or editor of each publication.

Selecting and Acquiring Content

Traditionally, scholarly publishers acquire work based on its compatibility with their disciplinary strengths, its scholarly merit, the prestige of the author, and its potential market, among other considerations. Library publishers may be guided by markedly different criteria. David Seaman, dean of libraries and university librarian at Syracuse University Libraries, explains, "Librarians have a strong service ethic. When we're approached, our inclination isn't to say no. If there's a need, we are willing partners" (personal communication, February 17, 2017). This tendency makes it all the more important for libraries to establish thoughtful parameters for projects that they take on in order to avoid overcommitting and overpromising. Clear policies ensure that the library makes strategic, fair, and transparent decisions about its investments of time and resources. Determining selection or eligibility criteria is therefore a paramount concern for new and growing library publishers.

The fundamental questions concern the type of author and the type of content your library will work with. Will your library publish any author or only those affiliated with your campus? Will you work with graduate and undergraduate students? Will you have a specific editorial focus or publish work on any topic? Policies on these issues vary widely depending on an individual library's capacity and mission.

Many libraries will work only with faculty and students who have an affiliation with their campus. This approach may seem anathema, particularly to those in university press publishing, who assiduously avoid publishing their own faculty's work. However, it aligns with libraries' mandate to serve their campus community and steward its research outputs. A publishing program designed in this way can become an effective marketing tool for the university, showcasing the variety of intellectual work of faculty and students. Other library publishers have explicitly embraced working with faculty members from any university. The University of Pittsburgh, for example, will consider publishing any faculty-run journal, regardless of institutional affiliation, as long as the editors are amenable to OA publication (Perry, Borchert, Deliyannides, Kosavic, & Kennison, 2011, p. 200). Many libraries also choose to work with graduate students and even undergraduates (usually supervised by a faculty advisor) to produce student research journals or other publications. Whether you choose to publish only faculty affiliated with your campus or all comers, or anything in between, clearly determining and advertising who is eligible to publish with you can help your program grow sustainably and coherently.

Library publishers must also consider their editorial focus. Commercial publishers and university presses typically build lists or portfolios of publications in a certain discipline. A strong list establishes a publisher's reputation in a given area, generating prestige and attracting new authors and readers. Because of their unique business model, many libraries choose not to specialize, accepting any scholarly or creative content that meets their eligibility criteria. Others choose to focus on specific disciplines (e.g., existing research strengths of their institution) or on topics of local or regional interest. Libraries report specializing in disciplines as diverse as geology, disability studies, and education (LPC Directory Committee, 2016). Xia (2009) proposes disrupting the discipline-based publishing model altogether, suggesting that North American libraries should consider publishing discipline-agnostic megajournals of faculty work, a model common among Chinese universities.

In addition to institutional affiliation and subject matter, library publishers may consider establishing a range of additional overarching parameters that apply to all publications in their portfolio. Such criteria might include only publishing content that uses Creative Commons licenses, expecting journals to publish a minimum number of articles per calendar year, or requiring that all publications undergo peer review. Some library publishers have an editorial board that oversees the program and approves works for publications, but this may not always be possible for small or growing publishers. For the purposes of ensuring academic rigor, some libraries require authors or editors to identify their method of quality control up front (whether peer review or otherwise) and include letters of endorsement from other faculty at the institution. These steps help address potential concerns about publishing unsuitable content.

Defining a Service Model

Library publishers provide a range of services related to editing, production, marketing and discovery, assessment, and preservation of scholarly and creative works. Core services often build on libraries' traditional strengths in access, discovery, and preservation, but libraries are also providing support for the editorial, production, and business management processes. In addition to maintaining a publishing platform, libraries often manage the peer-review workflow, provide or arrange copyediting for manuscripts, and prepare contracts and licenses. Production services include activities such as graphic design and typesetting, compiling indexes, and facilitating print-on-demand services (either in-house or through a third-party vendor). Libraries support marketing and discovery by providing cataloging and metadata services, notifying relevant abstracting and indexing services and aggregators, assigning DOIs or other permanent identifiers, registering ISSNs and ISBNs, and monitoring analytics. Given their experience as educators, librarians also frequently provide training and guidance to authors and editors on everything from using the publishing platform to crafting a copyright policy. Finally, libraries offer a range of support for multimedia and other supplemental content. For example, they may offer dataset management, audio/video streaming, or digitization services.

Many libraries offer tiered or à la carte services. Kennison (2011) describes the tiered service model at Columbia University Libraries' Center for Digital Research and Scholarship, which ranges from "free bare-bones service . . . offering only installation of the software and ongoing hosting" to a premium service that offers "comprehensive set up, configuration, training, and design support, including logo design . . . multiple layout options, and incorporation of complex graphical elements, such as inclusion of an embedded video player" (pp. 202–203).

From the first interaction with authors and editors, library publishers should make clear the extent and nature of the services they provide. Authors and editors may be accustomed to an entirely different relationship with their publisher and may come in with unrealistic or incorrect expectations. Roh finds that authors often come in wanting "beautiful, copy-edited, print publications, even though that's not what they value as readers. I've had to learn how to tell them that's not what we do, but in a way that's not discouraging" (personal communication, February 1, 2017). Xia (2009) notes that surveys and anecdotal evidence support the notion that, in general, "scholars have a positive attitude toward cooperating with librarians and are willing to take the responsibility of organizing an editorial process for the quality control of publications" (p. 372). Green of UIUC argues that even mainstream scholarly publishers have always relied on considerable faculty participation (e.g., as volunteer reviewers) and have increasingly shifted responsibilities for rights clearance and even copyediting to their authors and editors (personal communication, January 30, 2017).

Formalizing Roles and Responsibilities
After roles and responsibilities have been negotiated, they are ideally elaborated and formalized in a memorandum of understanding (MOU) or a hosting agreement. The MOU should clearly define the specific roles and responsibilities of the publisher and author or editor(s) and may also include details

about the publication and its policies. At the Claremont Colleges Library, for example, the library explicitly takes responsibility for the functional aspects of publishing, committing to "maintain the publishing platform; assist with initial journal/article design; establish basic editorial standards; assist with policy development; register ISSN and DOIs; assist with article publication; assist with indexing applications/contracts; deliver content to indexers/databases; and preservation" (Swift, n.d., p. 6). Authors and editors are broadly responsible for content and are charged with "oversight of content development (working with authors and making publication decisions); management of peer review process; [an] awareness/enforcement of relevant legal and ethical policies (for authors, reviewers, editors); ensuring sustained publication on a regular schedule; communicat[ing] with editorial board on a regular basis; [and] maintain[ing] collaboration and communication with publisher" (Swift, n.d., p. 7).

Libraries, as the stewards of the publication, should also consider addressing questions of sustainability, continuity, and preservation. For how long (and under what conditions) will you commit to actively supporting a publication? For how long will you commit to simply hosting the content? What happens if the journal editor leaves your campus or when a new editor is appointed? The extensive list of questions to consider may seem daunting, but Seaman encourages libraries to fully appreciate the intensive nature of journal publishing. He finds widespread "naivete early on about [the] burden of journal publishing with its complex series of deadlines with various authors" as opposed to monograph publishing, which tends to deal with one author and is done once the book is published (personal communication, February 17, 2017).

Developing Publication-Specific Policies

In consultation with the library, each author or editor must also consider a laundry list of questions that vary based on the type of publication. For journals, editors face a litany of decisions, from determining who will own copyright on published articles to selecting a preferred citation style (Ho, 2013). Eve (2012) recommends, at a minimum, that editors must establish the "journal name(!), scope and remit; OA policy (I'd recommend Creative Commons Attribution) and copyright stance (let your authors keep their copyright); publishing mode (issues or rolling? Do issues always make sense in an online environment, or should you just publish as submissions arrive?); initial CFP [call for papers]; [and] timing (don't time it so that all your first submissions arrive in the Christmas break, when nobody can review them, for example)."

Each publication requires an author agreement that may consist largely of boilerplate text but also may require tailoring to the policies and practices of each publication. Schlosser (2014) recommends developing a flexible, modular author agreement that ensures some standardization between publications but can be easily modified to suit the needs of individual authors or editors. A standard agreement she helped develop at Ohio State University is designed to be modular, "with sections that can be added or removed to support various licensing arrangements (like Creative Commons) and submission procedures," and supports modifications on a case-by-case basis. For example, the agreement was modified at the request of a student journal to require acceptance by both the student author and the student's advisor. Another modification added a provision "for an author who wanted to exempt the images in her submission from the Creative Commons license that was applied to the text" (Schlosser, 2014).

Working through pages of decisions and arcane policy questions with authors and editors can be one of the most time-consuming aspects of publishing, according to Allegra Swift of the Claremont Colleges Library. She explains, "Many faculty editors are new to the publishing process. They have published articles in journals, but have never been on the other side. Spending time working with editors on their policies, and making sure policies and other information is up-to-date on the journal's website takes a lot of time" (personal communication, February 20, 2017).

Recommended Reading and Resources
- The University of Michigan (http://wiki.publishing.umich.edu/Publishing _Agreements) and the Ohio State University (https://library.osu.edu/ blogs/digitalscholarship/2014/10/03/standard-author-agreement-for -journal-publishing/) have publicly posted author agreements that may serve as useful models. Legal documents such as author agreements should always be vetted by university counsel to ensure compliance with and suitability to your institution's individual policies.

- Emory University has also spearheaded the Mellon-funded initiative to develop a modular publishing agreement tailored to the specific challenges of publishing digital scholarship. The model agreements are available at https://www.modelpublishingcontract.org/.
- The University of Texas at Austin (https://uta-ir.tdl.org/uta-ir/handle/10106/25649) and the University of South Florida (http://scholarcommons.usf.edu/tlar/10/) have publicly posted journal hosting agreements/MOUs. Legal documents such as MOUs should be vetted by university counsel to ensure compliance with and suitability to your institution's individual policies.
- Ho (2013) offers an excellent checklist of issues for library publishers and journal editors. The questions in his checklist serve as a practical starting point for developing service agreements and memoranda of understanding between libraries and their partners.
- The PKP School has developed a platform-agnostic, modular curriculum to train new journal editors: http://pkpschool.sfu.ca/becoming-an -editor/.

DISCOVERY AND MARKETING

Okerson and Holzman (2015) observe, "Today, anybody with a website can publish in the sense of organizing and presenting (meticulously or casually) a body of information and ideas. It is harder to find the metaphorical shop window where readers will discover it" (p. 19). University press and commercial scholarly publishers have a significant advantage in this regard. Their well-established brands, reputations, and networks get the attention of potential buyers and readers. They spend considerable time and resources promoting their publications through the appropriate channels and connecting them with the right readers. The questions for libraries, according to Green of UIUC are, "How do we give our authors the same impact? How do we make library publishing viable not simply because it's lightweight and flexible, but because it is a way to get your work out there powerfully?" (personal communication, January 30, 2017). Simply storing content, whether print or digital, is no longer enough. Libraries have increasingly embraced a mandate to promote access, discovery, use, and creation. Library publishing should be no exception.

Most library publishers lack the staffing and resources to undertake many traditional marketing activities, such as advertising, having a booth at disciplinary conferences, or even running e-mail marketing campaigns. They may have insufficient time and expertise to ensure that their publications are listed in the proper subject indexes and promoted to the appropriate disciplinary organization. Even getting listed in the most obvious discovery channels can prove elusive. Library publishers frequently report difficulty getting their own libraries to produce catalog records for their publications. The Directory of Open Access Journals (DOAJ), ostensibly a natural fit, routinely rejects library-published journals based on extensive and intensive journal quality requirements that set a bar that many library publishers cannot reach. Beyond the technical and resource issues, libraries may struggle to establish a marketable identity. A single library publishing program may publish indiscriminately in a range of disciplines and often disseminates a range of publication types, from gray literature to peer-reviewed journals. Given this lack of editorial focus, Rapple (2015) asks, "Is it possible to create a focused brand identity when one core expression of brand, your products, may be so diverse as to defy easy unification, however consistent your visual expression, cultural characteristics, etc.?" Library publishers rarely benefit from the same economies of scale or well-curated lists that allow commercial publishers to expertly target their audiences.

> LIBRARY PUBLISHERS FREQUENTLY REPORT DIFFICULTY GETTING THEIR OWN LIBRARIES TO PRODUCE CATALOG RECORDS FOR THEIR PUBLICATIONS.

Library publishers frequently undertake informal (e.g., hosting gray literature and undergraduate journals) and formal (e.g., peer-reviewed faculty journals and monographs) publishing efforts side by side. Differentiating the products of each distinct activity presents an additional challenge. At Pacific University, where a self-publishing imprint that publishes content without peer review coexists with a formal university press with traditional editorial processes, Isaac Gilman finds it challenging but critical to make sure potential authors and readers don't conflate the two (personal communication, January 30, 2017). The press's mission is, in part, to raise the profile and prestige of the institution, while the self-publishing services respond to the faculty's need to disseminate nontraditional and informal publications. With two distinct identities, these services risk undermining one another without careful communication and positioning.

Marketing remains underresearched and underutilized among library publishers. However, a few approaches and examples are worth highlighting here. Okerson and Holzman (2015) recommend that libraries "learn how to construct metadata so as to enhance a work's chances of appearing prominently on a search in its subject" (p. 20). They suggest that productive partnerships could be forged with metadata and cataloging librarians to study best practices. Okerson and Holzman (2015) further recommend that libraries leverage social media to broadly promote their work in addition to honing in on the often extremely specific audiences who might be interested in niche publishing. They also contend that the flipped business model of OA publishing, in which the library publisher "elicits sustaining commitments" from institutional funders rather than "recruiting subscribers" to pay for content, demands an increasing focus on internal marketing and advocacy. Word-of-mouth and in-person networking remain popular, even in a digital world. Library publishers may consider joining a journal editor at a disciplinary conference to present or simply network. Working with liaison librarians, who may have intimate knowledge of the appropriate professional associations, publications, e-mail lists, and other promotional venues, can also be a productive strategy that leverages the library's existing expertise.

Recommended Reading and Resources

- As part of its journal editor training curriculum, the PKP School details a variety of strategies for promoting OA journals through a range of channels, from word of mouth to social media. See http://pkpschool .sfu.ca/becoming-an-editor/module-9/unit-4-developing-promotional -strategies/.
- Taylor & Francis regularly blogs about marketing strategies for journal editors. Despite the differences in scale and strategy, much of the advice can translate to the library publishing context. See http:// editorresources.taylorandfrancisgroup.com/tag/marketing/.

BUSINESS MODELS AND SUSTAINABILITY

Determining appropriate funding models for scholarly publishing remains a significant topic of debate within and beyond the library publishing community. The OA movement has empowered the academy to devise new, and some argue more efficient, funding models that ensure the continued viability of academic publishing in an evolving marketplace.

Who Should Pay?

Isaac Gilman of Pacific University Libraries explains, "One of the biggest questions for library publishing is sustainability, and part of that is deciding who should pay and convincing them to do so" (personal communication, January 30, 2017). The central question comes down to who should bear the cost burden for publishing. Should the university cover all the costs through subsidies? Should individual authors contribute through article processing charges? Should broader consortia or coalitions of libraries band together to fund publishing at scale? Should private foundations or technology start-ups play a role? Are there still instances when readers or subscribers should pay? There are examples of business models that engage each of the above funding strategies and others. Among the majority of library publishers in North America, institutional subsidies provide the vast majority of funding. Nearly half of library publishers rely exclusively on the library's operating budget for their funding, while the majority draw at least some of their funding from this source (LPC Directory Committee, 2016). Seven percent draw at least some funding from the library's materials budget, redirecting resources from purchasing content to producing it (LPC Directory Committee, 2016). By contrast, only 17 of the more than 100 institutions inventoried in the *Library Publishing Directory 2017* generate revenue from sales or licensing, while 7 institutions charge users for their services (LPC Directory Committee, 2016).

Unlike most other scholarly publishers, the majority of libraries are not expected to generate any revenue, let alone break even or make a profit. This financial independence allows library publishers to pursue OA publishing without relying on an author fee model. It also allows libraries to take on projects that other publishers would consider cost prohibitive or unprofitable. Consider, for example, *The Ethics of Suicide Digital Archive* (https://ethicsofsuicide.lib.utah.edu/about/), a project of the University of Utah and Oxford University Press (OUP), which comprises a redacted 750-page print volume published by OUP and a web version of the full manuscript hosted by the University of Utah (Anderson, 2015). The entire 1,200-page volume would have been prohibitively expensive to produce and distribute in print but was an excellent candidate for digital publication. Running on an entirely subsidized model entails convincing university decision makers of the inherent value of the enterprise. Charlotte Roh of the University of San Francisco explains, "There's a big leap in perception from cost recovery to a service model. We don't have any plan to ever generate revenue. What that means is you have to commit money upfront and you're not going to get it back" (personal communication, February 1, 2017).

Institutional subsidies allow many library publishers to adopt fully OA publication models, a practice that also aligns with library values. As previously noted, creating a more open and equitable scholarly communication system is a strong motivator and an underlying principle for many library publishers. However, library publishers also cite more practical reasons for going OA. Gilman explains, "As soon as you start selling things, there's a whole other slate of legal and financial issues you have to consider" (personal communication, January 30, 2017). From assessing APCs or subscription fees to protecting content from piracy, generating revenue entails myriad considerations that may be more trouble than they are worth, especially at the small scale of most library publishing programs.

There are, however, many examples of library publishers (or their journals) successfully covering costs by selling subscriptions. Busher and Kamotsky (2016) recount the example of the *Journal of Outdoor Recreation, Education, and Leadership*, which found a home in the institutional repository at Western Kentucky University after the journal's editors balked at the high publishing fees commercial scholarly publishers had quoted. The journal covers its costs by selling subscriptions and, as of 2016, has published six volumes. Early publishing efforts at Columbia University also experimented with revenue generation. "Columbia Earthscape: an Online Resource on the Global Environment" employed a subscription model predicated on offering the resource at the "lowest possible price that will allow for sustainability" (Wittenberg, 2001, p. 30).

Libraries that choose to pursue cost recovery often opt for hybrid models. For example, a library may make a publication openly available online but charge for a print or print-on-demand version. Alternatively, a library might make a basic version of a publication free but restrict supplemental or premium content to paying customers. Some library publishers charge modest fees for their services to individual authors or to an author or editor's center or department. Tiered service models, which allow authors and editors to select the specific level of support they require, show particular promise. The University of North Texas (UNT) Libraries' Eagle Editions, for example, offers a variable fee structure for all its publications (Hawkins, 2015). A small flat fee covers basic online publication (light proofreading, hosting in UNT's repository, DOI assignment, and cataloging). Additional paid services such as custom cover design and rights management can be added at the author's or editor's discretion.

Libraries are also exploring a range of other funding models that cover the costs of publication up front rather than passing the burden along to consumers, such as fundraising through alumni networks or friends of the library groups. David Seaman of Syracuse University Libraries explains, "When you put your mind to it, there are considerable fundraising opportunities for libraries to explore through their alumni networks" (personal communication, February 20, 2017). Seaman observes that university presses have successfully recruited individual donors to sponsor content, underwriting the cost of publication because they are interested in scholarly dissemination in general or convinced of the importance of the publication. The key, Seaman argues, is selling content rather than infrastructure. Donors can more easily see the value of sponsoring a publication and can assess the impact of their contribution by looking at download counts, citation rates, and reviews. Investment in infrastructure, such as funding the development of an institutional repository, is less glamorous and harder to value.

What Does It Cost?

Library publishing programs rarely launch with a full-fledged budget or a fleet of new staff. Rather, they often begin by reallocating staff time and repurposing existing infrastructure and scale up slowly over time. This approach not only allows time to develop proficiency in the variety of publishing workflows; it can be a useful way of gauging costs and capacity before making a significant investment. Royster (2014) commends this approach, advising libraries to control costs at the outset, as "nothing attracts supervision as fast as funding" (p. 105). According to Royster (2014), it is advantageous to "start small and build up; it is much easier to grow than to scale down" (p. 105).

Whether or not libraries intend to recoup their investments, estimating the basic cost of running a publishing program may be useful in planning for sustainability. Given that many library publishing programs are embedded within and blended with other library operations, determining the exact costs of supporting a publishing program may prove difficult. Publishing programs often rely largely on existing library staff and infrastructure, which may not exclusively support publishing initiatives. However, headway has been made in recent years to estimate the direct and indirect costs of producing certain types of publications. Walters and Hilton (2015, p. 49) identified an average cost of $27,000 to publish a monograph at two presses: Indiana University Press and Michigan Publishing Services. This cost includes acquisitions, editorial work, and intensive marketing, some of the most time-consuming and expensive processes that scholarly publishers engage in. Most library publishers eschew these activities and therefore assume only direct production costs in addition to their overhead, meaning total costs may be significantly lower. An Ithaka S+R study of a larger cohort of university presses similarly identified a minimum cost of around $16,000 to publish a monograph (Maron, Mulhern, Rossman, & Schmelzinger, 2016). Luminos OA, the open access imprint of the University of California Press estimates a baseline cost of $15,000 (Lockett & Speicher, 2016). Open Book Publishers, a born-digital OA publisher based in the United Kingdom, estimates that it costs around $8,000 to produce the first copy of a book—in other words, the costs associated with acquiring, editing, and producing the monograph, but not printing or distributing it (Gatti & Mierowsky, 2016).

Publishing journals, conference proceedings, and gray literature is generally significantly less expensive. At its most basic, this type of publication requires little more than a repository and a workflow for ingesting content. Much of the labor costs in OA journal publishing (e.g., editing, peer review, submission management, and marketing) are shouldered by the editors of the publication, not by the publisher. OA journal publishers have become increasingly transparent about their costs, largely in the interest of justifying article processing charges, providing a helpful baseline for library publishers.

Van Noorden (2013, p. 427) reported that the large OA publisher Hindawi cites a cost of $290 per article, while the researcher-led Ubiquity Press estimates its average per-article cost at $300. Martin Eve (2017) of the Open Library of the Humanities (OLH) estimated their cost per article at £101.50 (US$126.56) and the total fixed costs of operating the OLH at £182,079.60 (US$227,036.87).

Recommended Reading and Resources

- In 2016, a team at Ithaka S+R, led by Nancy Maron (Maron, Mulhern, Rossman, & Schmelzinger, 2016), published the results of a study that aimed to estimate direct and in-kind costs of publishing monographs. The results of their study serve as a useful guide.
- Martin Paul Eve's (2017) breakdown of the costs of running the Open Library of the Humanities, which resembles in many ways a library publishing program, provides an excellent budgeting primer for future journal publishers.
- Gatti and Mierowsky's (2016) report on the operating cost of Open Book Publishers (OBP) may be particularly useful for estimating monograph publishing costs. Much like many library publishers, OBP was born digital, is open access, and emphasizes lightweight workflows.

CRITIQUES AND DEBATES

This section addresses two influential debates within the library publishing community. The twin questions of "should libraries publish?" and "can we call what libraries do publishing?" get at the role of the 21st-century library in the contexts of the university and the information economy.

SHOULD LIBRARIES PUBLISH?

The typical library budget is flat or declining, new staff positions can be hard to come by, and libraries face no shortage of new demands on their time and capacity, from taking on campus data management support to developing information literacy programs that address the needs of 21st-century learners. Is it wise, in this context, to take on another auxiliary function? Is it strategic to prioritize publishing when making difficult decisions about resource allocation? As Xia (2009) observes, "A library publishing program . . . requires a long-term commitment and considerable investment of the library's resources, which will inevitably divert its limited funds and personnel from other endeavours" (p. 22).

Whether or not libraries should publish depends in part on how we define publishing. Isaac Gilman argues that "if, at [the] most basic level, the idea is that libraries will remain involved in helping faculty and students create and disseminate content, that will continue to grow" (personal communication, January 30, 2017). Libraries have increasingly shifted their priorities from collection to creation through the development of new services that support digital scholarship, "making" (e.g., 3-D print labs and other prototyping environments), reuse and remixing of content, and other forms of scholarly and creative production. Publishing fits neatly into this portfolio and can often be accomplished in partnership with these other services.

Libraries have demonstrated the capacity and interest to play a more active role in content creation. Does that interest inevitably lead to all libraries becoming publishers? In their seminal discussion of the academy's role in 21st-century publishing, Brown, Griffiths, and Rascoff (2007) argue that "every university that produces research should have a publishing strategy, but that does not mean that it should have a 'press.'" Establishing a press (or a significant library publishing operation) is no simple endeavor. Library publishers need a strong rationale for publishing (stemming from a careful assessment of institutional needs) coupled with the right combination of staffing, expertise, partnerships, funding, institutional commitment, and campus interest.

Without an institutional commitment and appropriate resources, library publishing programs may wither or flounder. Even those that successfully complete projects risk producing amateurish results. Disseminating low-quality publications may harm the image of the institution or the library and beg the question of whether publishing is a worthwhile use of library resources. Some also argue that this type of publishing may hurt scholarly communication more than it helps. Allegra Swift of the Claremont Colleges Library contends that libraries should only become publishers if they have the "bandwidth, focus, and support" to ensure they produce high-quality publications (personal communication, February 20, 2017). She argues, "If libraries are just churning out lots of low-quality content, we're not helping anything." Amateurish OA publications contribute to perceptions that OA scholarship has less value and that OA venues are the option of last resort for scholarship that fails to meet the standards of commercial publishing.

Libraries have a wealth of other opportunities to advance OA scholarship and support faculty needs without actually becoming publishers. Librarians can guide faculty to external sources of support and encourage OA publishing. They can also fund the initiatives at the forefront of innovative OA publishing models, such as Lever Press, Knowledge Unlatched, or the Open Library of the Humanities. They also have other means of supporting a more open, equitable, and innovative scholarly publishing system by educating and advising their faculty and students. Walters (2012) projects one future scenario for library publishing in which libraries are principally consultants and advisors, educating faculty and students on copyright and OA publication, helping them select appropriate publishing opportunities, and partnering with university presses and commercial publishers on issues of mutual importance such as digital preservation and discovery. For many libraries, this role may be the most productive use of resources.

If libraries do intend to stake a claim in the publishing ecosystem, they need to convince a broad range of constituents and observers—including campus administrators, university presses, librarians, commercial publishers, and faculty—that library publishing is an important, strategic, and purposeful service area. They must demonstrate a commitment to programmatic, sustainable, and ongoing efforts.

IS IT REALLY PUBLISHING?

Intimately tied to the question of whether libraries *should* publish is whether what libraries are doing can be called publishing. Some contend that libraries are hosts or service providers, but not publishers, given that they often eschew the intensive *processes* of acquisition, editing, typesetting, and other hallmarks of the work that publishers do. Anderson (2016) identifies at least 96 discrete activities, from "audience/field detection and cultivation" to "responding to legal actions," that he argues are integral to being a publisher. In the title of a 2013 blog post for the *Scholarly Kitchen*, Joe Esposito provocatively asked, "What is publishing if even a library can do it?" Esposito's skepticism about what libraries are doing and why they call it publishing is rooted in the argument that publishing involves more than making content public. "Hundreds of libraries now have publishing programs, though the definition of 'publishing' is not always clear and often seems to mean (in this context) 'dissemination'" (Esposito, 2013). Esposito proposes that libraries are "service providers" rather than publishers, contending, like Anderson (2016), that the identity of publishing is inseparable from its processes. Royster (2014) compiled several quotes from a 2013 Association of American University Presses (AAUP) report on library–university press collaboration. One press representative argues, "[In] our library's digital publishing group there is simply no knowledge of publishing. It's one thing to create content or even package it. That doesn't mean you're publishing" (p. 97).

Early on, Courant (2007) advanced a counterargument, contending that publishing is nothing more than the "business of making scholarly things public." Shirky (2012) infamously contended that publishing is now a button. Does lowering the barriers to publication or expanding its definition necessarily mean we devalue it? Charlotte Roh, scholarly communication librarian at the University of San Francisco, argues, "Publishing has become less precious. We're not monks hand-copying manuscripts. That doesn't mean it has become disposable. It's just a more public, accessible process" (personal communication, January 31, 2017). Given their expertise with information literacy, technology, and education, librarians may be particularly well suited to supporting authors and editors in this new environment.

> PUSHING THE BOUNDARIES OF WHAT IS CONSIDERED PUBLISHING MAY IN FACT BE ONE OF LIBRARY PUBLISHING'S GREATEST STRENGTHS.

Pushing the boundaries of what is considered publishing may in fact be one of library publishing's greatest strengths. As noted earlier, libraries explicitly embrace experimental publications, media-rich content, and content that is otherwise neglected. Finally, some dismiss semantic arguments altogether. Whether or not what libraries do "counts" as publishing makes little difference if they are fulfilling their mission.

FINAL THOUGHTS

Library publishing addresses critical needs on campus and in the scholarly publishing marketplace. As a campus service, it aligns well with the values and skills at the core of the library profession and represents a strategic means of fulfilling the library's commitment to access and stewardship. It is a natural complement to institutional repositories, data curation, digital scholarship, scholarly communications, and information literacy programs and often leverages the existing skills and networks of librarians to build deeper partnerships. In the marketplace, library publishing addresses unmet needs and gaps that other publishers are uninterested in filling. Library publishing provides a home for content that might not otherwise see the light of day, regardless of its scholarly merit or potential impact. From gray literature and student work, to journals on arcane topics, to encyclopedic collections of primary source material, libraries embrace the unprofitable, the informal, and the esoteric. Their entrepreneurial bent also provides space for experimentation, producing new and innovative publications that leverage the possibilities of networked information.

No matter how lightweight the workflows or how lean the staffing, viable library publishing requires a considerable investment, planning, and iteration. It also requires deep and mutually beneficial partnerships with stakeholders on campus and off. The growth of library publishing as a strong and sustainable field requires the development of a robust community to share best practices, undertake research of mutual interest, and promote the interests of library publishers.

While not all libraries will find that publishing aligns with their service portfolios or their institutional missions, there are a wealth of ways they can contribute to a more open and innovative scholarly communications environment. In their roles as advisors and educators, they can continue to provide guidance to their communities. They can also redirect resources from collecting commercial publications to supporting new OA initiatives. Finally, they can partner with other publishers on and off their campuses. Libraries' relationships with university presses, whether or not they are on the same campus, can be particularly fruitful.

Over the past few decades, library publishing has emerged as a distinctive subfield of publishing, complete with its own values, priorities, and practices. In his influential book *Books in a Digital Age*, sociologist John Thompson (2005) elaborates the idea that publishing cannot be adequately characterized as one monolithic field. Thompson proposes that publishing can be best understood as a set of distinct fields, each with its own unique "logic," which Thompson explains is "the outcome of a specific set of forces and pressures which shapes the activities of particular agents and organizations" (2005, p. 6). Library publishing and its measures of success, its challenges, its potential, and its best practices are therefore most productively evaluated not in comparison to other scholarly publishers but rather in how they infuse library values and take into account libraries' unique circumstances. Even within the subfield of library publishing, a diverse range of models has taken root, reflecting the creativity and ingenuity of librarians responding to transformations on their own campuses and throughout the ecosystem of scholarly publishing.

RECOMMENDED READING

JOURNALS

- *Journal of Electronic Publishing* (http://journalofelectronicpublishing.org)
- *Journal of Librarianship and Scholarly Communications* (http://jlsc-pub.org)
- *Journal of Scholarly Publishing* (http://www.utpjournals.press/loi/jsp)
- *Learned Publishing* (http://www.alpsp.org/Learned-Publishing)

MONOGRAPHS AND REPORTS

- Bonn, M., & Furlough, M. (Eds.). (2015). *Getting the word out: Academic libraries as scholarly publishers.* Chicago, IL: Association of College and Research Libraries (ACRL).
- Brown, A. P. (2013). *Library publishing toolkit.* Geneseo, NY: IDS Project Press (SUNY Geneseo).
- Brown, L., Griffiths, R., Rascoff, M., & Guthrie, K. (2007). University publishing in a digital age. *Journal of Electronic Publishing, 10*(3). http://dx.doi.org/10.3998/3336451.0010.301
- Davis-Kahl, S., & M. Henley (Eds.). (2013). *Common ground at the nexus of information literacy and scholarly communication.* Chicago, IL: ACRL.

- Hahn, K. (2008). *Research library publishing services: New options for university publishing*. Washington, DC: Association of Research Libraries (ARL). Retrieved from http://www.arl.org/bm~doc/research-library-publishing-services.pdf

BLOGS AND WEBSITES

- DH+Lib (http://acrl.ala.org/dh/)
- Library Publishing Coalition (LPC; http://www.librarypublishing.org)
- Martin Paul Eve's personal blog (https://www.martineve.com/)
- PKP School (http://pkpschool.sfu.ca/)
- *The Scholarly Kitchen* (http://scholarlykitchen.sspnet.org)

REFERENCES

AAUP. (2013). *Press and library collaboration survey* [PDF document]. Retrieved from http://www.aaupnet.org/images/stories/data/librarypresscollaboration_report _corrected.pdf

AAUP. (2016). AAUP snapshot [Web page]. Retrieved from http://www.aaupnet.org/about -aaup/about-university-presses/aaup-snapshot

Anderson, K. (2016, February 1). Guest post: Kent Anderson updated—96 things publishers do (2016 edition) [Blog post]. Retrieved from https://scholarlykitchen.sspnet .org/2016/02/01/guest-post-kent-anderson-updated-96-things-publishers-do-2016 -edition/

Anderson, R. (2015, September 15). Library publishing redux: An unprecedented example of a scholar/library/publisher partnership [Blog post]. Retrieved from https:// scholarlykitchen.sspnet.org/2015/09/15/library-publishing-redux-an-unprecedented -example-of-a-scholarlibrarypublisher-partnership/

Björk, B.-C., & Solomon, D. (2013). The publishing delay in scholarly peer-reviewed journals. *Journal of Informetrics, 7*(4), 914–923. http://dx.doi.org/10.1016/j.joi.2013 .09.001

Bonn, M., & Furlough, M. (Eds.). (2015). *Getting the word out: Academic libraries as scholarly publishers*. Chicago, IL: Association of College and Research Libraries (ACRL).

Brown, A. P. (2013). *Library publishing toolkit*. Geneseo, NY: IDS Project Press (SUNY Geneseo).

Brown, L., Griffiths, R., Rascoff, M., & Guthrie, K. (2007). University publishing in a digital age. *Journal of Electronic Publishing, 10*(3). http://dx.doi.org/10.3998/3336451 .0010.301

Busher, C., & Kamotsky, I. (2015). Stories and statistics from library-led publishing. *Learned Publishing, 28*(1), 64–68. Advance online publication. Retrieved from http://works .bepress.com/cgi/viewcontent.cgi?article=1006&context=casey_busher

Carlin, R. (2016). Building a list. *Against the Grain, 28*(6). Retrieved from http:// www.against-the-grain.com/2017/01/v28-6-building-a-list/

Corbett, H., Ghaphery, J., Work, L., & Byrd, S. (2016). Choosing a repository platform: Open source vs. hosted solutions. In B. B. Callicott, D. Scherer, & A. Wesolek (Eds.), *Making institutional repositories work*. West Lafayette, IN: Purdue University Press. Advance online publication. Retrieved from http://scholarscompass.vcu.edu/libraries _pubs/33

Courant, P. (2007). Why I hate the phrase "scholarly communication" [Blog post]. Retrieved from http://paulcourant.net/2007/11/23/why-i-hate-the-phrase-scholarly -communication/

Duckett, K., & Warren, S. (2013). Exploring the intersections of information literacy and scholarly communication: Two frames of reference for undergraduate instruction. In S. Davis-Kahl & M. Henley (Eds.), *Common ground at the nexus of information literacy and scholarly communication*. Chicago, IL: ACRL.

Elliott, M. A. (2015). The future of the monograph in the digital era: A report to the Andrew W. Mellon Foundation. *Journal of Electronic Publishing, 18*(4).

Esposito, J. (2013). Are university presses better than they were four years ago? [Blog post]. Retrieved from https://www.insidehighered.com/views/2013/06/21/are-university -presses-better-they-were-4-years-ago

Eve, M. P. (2012). Starting an open access journal: A step-by-step guide part 1 [Blog post]. Retrieved from https://www.martineve.com/2012/07/10/starting-an-open-access -journal-a-step-by-step-guide-part-1/

Eve, M. P. (2017). How much does it cost to run a small scholarly publisher? [Blog post]. Retrieved from https://www.martineve.com/2017/02/13/how-much-does-it-cost-to -run-a-small-scholarly-publisher/

Furlough, M. (2011). The publisher in the library. In S. Walter & K. Williams (Eds.), *The expert library: Staffing, sustaining, and advancing the academic library in the 21st century*. Chicago, IL: ACRL. Advance online publication. Retrieved from http://www.personal .psu.edu/mjf25/blogs/on_furlough/2010/11/18/Furlough-Publisher_in_Library -ExpertLibrary_Chapter08-preprint.pdf

Gatti, R., & Mierowsky, M. (2016). Funding open access monographs: A coalition of libraries and publishers. *College & Research Libraries News, 77*(9), 456–459. https://doi.org/ 10.5860/crln.77.9.9557

Gilman, I. (2015). Adjunct no more: Promoting scholarly publishing as a core service of academic libraries. *Against the Grain, 26*(6). Advance online publication. Retrieved from http://commons.pacificu.edu/cgi/viewcontent.cgi?article=1026&context=libfac

Hahn, K. (2008). *Research library publishing services: New options for university publishing*. Washington, DC: Association of Research Libraries (ARL). Retrieved from http://www .arl.org/bm~doc/research-library-publishing-services.pdf

Hawkins, K. (2015). A for-fee library-based publishing service [Poster]. Retrieved from https://digital.library.unt.edu/ark:/67531/metadc699786/

Ho, A. K. (2013). Library services for creating and publishing student research journals. *Library publishing toolkit*. A. P. Brown (Ed.). Geneseo, NY: IDS Project Press (SUNY Geneseo). Retrieved from http://opensuny.org/omp/index.php/IDSProject/catalog/book/25

Ivins, O., & Luther, J. (2011). *Publishing support for small print-based publishers: Options for ARL libraries*. Association of Research Libraries [PDF document]. Retrieved from http://www.arl.org/storage/documents/publications/pub-support_7mar11.pdf

Jones, P. (2014). What's going on in the library? Part 1: Librarian publishers may be more important than you think [Blog post]. Retrieved from https://scholarlykitchen.sspnet .org/2014/12/01/whats-going-on-in-the-library-part-1-librarian-publishers-may-be -more-important-than-you-think/

Kasdorf, W. (Ed.). (2003). *The Columbia guide to digital publishing*. New York: Columbia University Press.

Larivière, V., Haustein, S., & Mongeon, P. (2015). The oligopoly of academic publishers in the digital era. *PLOS ONE, 10*(6). https://doi.org/10.1371/journal.pone.0127502

LaRose, C., & Kahn, M. (2016). *Conducting a comprehensive survey of publishing activity at your institution* [PDF document]. Retrieved from https://deepblue.lib.umich.edu/ handle/2027.42/134688

Library Publishing Coalition. (2016). About us [Web page]. Retrieved from https:// librarypublishing.org/about-us

Library Publishing Coalition Directory Committee. (2016). *Library publishing directory 2017*. Atlanta, GA: Library Publishing Coalition. Retrieved from http://www .librarypublishing.org/resources/directory/lpd2017

Lippincott, S. K. (Ed.). (2014). *Library publishing directory 2015*. Atlanta, GA: Library Publishing Coalition. Retrieved from http://www.librarypublishing.org/resources/directory/ lpd2015

Lippincott, S. K. (Ed.). (2015). *Library publishing directory 2016*. Atlanta, GA: Library Publishing Coalition. Retrieved from http://www.librarypublishing.org/resources/directory/ lpd2016

Lippincott, S. K. (2016). The Library Publishing Coalition: Organizing libraries to enhance scholarly publishing. *Insights, 29*(2), 186–191. http://doi.org/10.1629/uksg.296

Lockett, A., & Speicher, L. (2016). New university presses in the UK: Accessing a mission. *Learned Publishing, 29*, 320–329. http://doi:10.1002/leap.1049

Lynch, C. (2003). Institutional repositories: Essential infrastructure for scholarship in the digital age. *ARL Bimonthly Report* (226), 1–7. Retrieved from https://www.cni.org/wp -content/uploads/2003/02/arl-br-226-Lynch-IRs-2003.pdf

Maron, N., Mulhern, C., Rossman, D., & Schmelzinger, K. (2016). *The costs of publishing monographs: Toward a transparent methodology*. New York: Ithaka S+R. https://doi.org/ 10.18665/sr.276785

McHale, M. (2011). Open access publishing with Drupal. *Code4Lib Journal* (15). Retrieved from http://journal.code4lib.org/articles/5913

Newfound Press. (n.d.). Newfound Press: A digital imprint of the University of Tennessee Libraries [Web page]. Retrieved from https://newfoundpress.utk.edu/

Newton, M. P., Bullock, D. M., Watkinson, C., Bracke, P. J., & Horton, D. K. (2011). Engaging new partners in transportation research: Integrating publishing, archiving, and indexing of technical literature into the research process [Preprint]. Retrieved from http://docs.lib.purdue.edu/lib_research/146

Okerson, A., & Holzman, A. (2015, July). The once and future publishing library. *Council on Library and Information Resources*. Retrieved from https://www.clir.org/pubs/reports/ pub166/Pub166-pdfORIG

Perry, A. M., Borchert, C. A., Deliyannides, T. S., Kosavic, A., Kennison, R., & Dyas-Correia, S. (2011). Libraries as journal publishers. *Serials Review, 37*(3).

PressBooks. (2017). For academia [Web page]. Retrieved from https://pressbooks.com/for
      -academia/

Rapple, C. (2015, December 10). What does brand mean for library-based presses? [Blog
      post]. Retrieved from https://scholarlykitchen.sspnet.org/2015/12/10/what-does-brand
      -mean-for-library-based-presses/

Robertson, W., & Simser, C. (2013). Managing e-publishing: Perfect harmony for serialists.
      Serials Librarian, 64, 118–128. http://dx.doi.org/10.1080/0361526X.2013.760399

Roh, C. (2014). Library-press collaborations: A study taken on behalf of the University of
      Arizona. *Journal of Librarianship and Scholarly Communication, 2*(4). https://doi.org/10
      .7710/2162-3309.1102

Roh, C. (2016). Library publishing and diversity values changing scholarly publishing
      through policy and scholarly communication education. *College & Research Libraries
      News, 77*(2), 82–85.

Royster, P. (2007). Publishing original content in an institutional repository. *Faculty Pub-
      lications, UNL Libraries.* Paper 126. Retrieved from http://digitalcommons.unl.edu/
      libraryscience/126

Royster, P. (2014). Library publishing is special: Selection and eligibility in library publish-
      ing. *Journal of Librarianship and Scholarly Communication, 2*(4). http://doi.org/10
      .7710/2162-3309.1183

Schlosser, M. (2014, October 3). Standard journal license agreement [Blog post]. Retrieved
      from https://library.osu.edu/blogs/digitalscholarship/2014/10/03/standard-author
      -agreement-for-journal-publishing/

Shirky, C. (2012, April 5). How we will read [Blog post]. Retrieved from https://web.archive
      .org/web/20140212200209/http://blog.findings.com/post/20527246081/how-we-will
      -read-clay-shirky

Skinner, K., Lippincott, S., Speer, J., & Walters, T. (2014). Library-as-publisher: Capac-
      ity building for the library publishing subfield. *Journal of Electronic Publishing, 17*(2).
      http://dx.doi.org/10.3998/3336451.0017.207

Smith, R. (2006). Peer review: A flawed process at the heart of science and journals. *Journal
      of the Royal Society of Medicine, 99*(4), 178–182. Retrieved from https://www.ncbi.nlm
      .nih.gov/pmc/articles/PMC1420798/

Sutton, S., & Chadwell, F. (2014). Open textbooks at Oregon State University: A case study
      of new opportunities for academic libraries and university presses. *Journal of Librarian-
      ship and Scholarly Communication, 2*(4). http://doi.org/10.7710/2162-3309.1174

Swift, A. (n.d.). *Roles and responsibilities* [PDF document]. Retrieved from http://libguides
      .libraries.claremont.edu/ld.php?content_id=12807478

Thomas, S. E. (2006). Publishing solutions for contemporary scholars: The library as
      innovator and partner. *Library Hi Tech, 24*(4), 563–573. http://dx.doi.org/10.1108/
      07378830610715428

Thompson, J. B. (2005). *Books in the digital age.* Cambridge, UK: Polity Press.

University of California Office of Scholarly Communication. (2014). Publishing tools [Web
      page]. Retrieved from http://osc.universityofcalifornia.edu/publishing-tools/

Van Noorden, R. (2013). Open access: The true cost of science publishing. *Nature, 495.*
      Retrieved from http://www.nature.com/news/open-access-the-true-cost-of-science
      -publishing-1.12676

Vinopal, J. (2012). Project portfolio management for academic libraries: A gentle introduc-
    tion. *College and Research Libraries, 73*(4).

Vinopal, J., & McCormick, M. (2013). Supporting digital scholarship in research libraries:
    Scalability and sustainability. *Journal of Library Administration, 53*(1), 27–42. http://dx
    .doi.org/10.1080/01930826.2013.756689

Wagner, A. B. (2010). Open access citation advantage: An annotated bibliography. *Issues in
    Science and Technology Librarianship, 60*(2). http://dx.doi.org/10.5062/F4Q81B0W

Walters, C., & Hilton, J. (2015). *A study of direct author subvention for publishing humanities
    books at two universities* [PDF document]. Retrieved from http://hdl.handle.net/2027
    .42/113671

Walters, T. (2012). The future role of publishing services in university libraries. *portal:
    Libraries and the Academy, 12*(4), 425–454.

Watkinson, C. (2016). Why marriage matters: A North American perspective on
    press/library partnerships. *Learned Publishing, 29*, 342–347. http://doi:10.1002/leap
    .1044

Weiner, S. A., & Watkinson, C. (2014). What do students learn from participation in an
    undergraduate research journal? Results of an assessment. *Journal of Librarianship and
    Scholarly Communication, 2*(2). http://doi.org/10.7710/2162-3309.1125

Welzenbach, R., & Colman, J. (2015). *Scaling up: Recovering costs to enable mission-driven
    library publishing* [PDF document]. Retrieved from http://hdl.handle.net/2027.42/
    111646

Werner, I. (2015). From services to partnering: A new strategy for OA publishing in Utrecht
    University Library [Blog post]. Retrieved from http://libereurope.eu/blog/2015/03/
    30/from-services-to-partnering-a-new-strategy-for-oa-publishing-in-utrecht-university
    -library/

Wittenberg, K. (2001). The Electronic Publishing Initiative at Columbia (EPIC): A
    university-based collaboration in digital scholarly communication. *Learned Publishing,
    14*, 29–32.

Xia, J. (2009). Library publishing as a new model of scholarly communication. *Journal of
    Scholarly Publishing, 40*(4), 370–383. http://dx.doi.org/10.1353/scp.0.0052

ABOUT THE AUTHOR

Sarah Lippincott is a librarian and consultant specializing in scholarly communication and digital scholarship. She served as the inaugural program director for the Library Publishing Coalition, a community-led membership association whose mission is to support a broad range of publishing activities in academic and research libraries. She received her MSLS from the University of North Carolina at Chapel Hill and her BA in the College of Letters and in French Studies from Wesleyan University. As a consultant, she has worked on strategic planning and communications for the Harvard Library, the Association of Research Libraries, SPARC, and the open access journal *eLife*.

www.ingramcontent.com/pod-product-compliance
Lightning Source LLC
Chambersburg PA
CBHW081251040426

42452CB00015B/2784